BON... ...HT

A SHORT HISTORY
OF THE
GUY FAWKES CELEBRATIONS

Jim Etherington

S. B. Publications

To the Bonfire Boys and Girls of Lewes
May they continue to keep alive the spirit of Bonfire

First published in 1993 by S.B. Publications
c/o 19 Grove Road, Seaford, East Sussex BN25 1TP

Reprinted in 1993

ISBN 1 85770 050 3

Typeset and Printed by Island Press Ltd
3 Cradle Hill Industrial Estate, Seaford, East Sussex BN25 3JE   Tel: 0323 490222

CONTENTS

Front cover: Cliffe Vikings processing down School Hill
(Photo: Phil Everitt)

Back cover: "Battle Axe", Cliffe Society 1980
(Photo: Phil Burcham)

Title page: The Cliffe Society's pioneer group in 1911 were dressed in the
uniforms of the Napoleonic period. Costumes during the early
years of this century often had a military flavour.

An exploding setpiece leads the Cliffe Bonfire Society down School Hill away from the War Memorial.
1986 was the last year the authorities permitted large rockets to be included in street firework displays.
(Photo: Leigh Simpson)

1. THE LEWES BONFIRE NIGHT CELEBRATIONS

Annually, on the evening of 5th November the principal streets of Lewes are thronged by thousands of inhabitants and visitors who have come to witness the celebrations held in the town to commemorate the Discovery of the Gunpowder Plot of 1605. Unlike the back-garden family affairs that are more typical of the rest of the country the annual 'Bonfire Night' celebrations in Lewes are a highly organised event which are carried out in a colourful and elaborate manner. Arranged by local clubs called 'Bonfire Societies' the celebrations involve large torchlit fancy dress processions accompanied by numerous bands, firework displays and bonfires. Such is the size and pageantry of the occasion that it has few parallels.

Cavaliers lead the Cliffe's procession in 1974. The following year the Society reverted to its now more customary Viking pioneer front.   (Photo: Sussex Express)

The celebrations are in reality five separate events, each organised by one of the five Lewes bonfire societies, Cliffe, Commercial Square, Lewes Borough, South Street Juvenile and Waterloo. Independent of each other they carry out their activities each 5th November in similar manner. The celebrations commence at five o'clock with the first processions of the various societies, followed by others which perambulate the High Street and adjacent roads at various intervals for the rest of the evening. Each society organizes its own processions in which its members

The 'dummy' effigy of Guy Fawkes being drawn on a trundle through the streets of Lewes. A second similar effigy packed with fireworks is ignited at each of the societies' firesite displays.

(Photo: Leigh Simpson)

8

parade wearing fancy dress costumes, carrying blazing paraffin soaked torches and accompanied by military, jazz and youth marching bands. The processions are headed by the badge of the Society and depending on the strength of the particular society, include between three and six hundred 'Bonfire Boys and Girls'.

During the early processions various ceremonies are enacted which, over the years have become intrinsic features of what the Bonfire Boys consider to be the traditions of the 'Fifth'. Each society throws a blazing tar barrel from Cliffe Bridge into the River Ouse, the precise origins of which remain elusive. All the societies lay a wreath at the town's war memorial to pay tribute to the Bonfire Boys who gave their lives in the two World Wars. The solemnity of the occasion is marked by two minutes silence, the playing of the Last Post and the rendering of a suitable hymn. Small firework displays, often in the shape of Flander's poppies are ignited during the service. Various other small firework set-pieces are ignited in the streets during the processions including a miniature replica of the Lewes Martyrs' Memorial that overlooks the town from Cliffe Hill.

The culmination of the early evening processions is the Grand United Procession that starts at the top of the High Street and processes the complete length of the town. All the Lewes societies, except Cliffe, take part and are joined by many visiting bonfire societies from the surrounding towns and villages who attend the Lewes celebrations supporting the various Lewes societies. Totalling over two thousand society members, accompanied by fifteen to twenty bands and being a mile or more in length, the procession can take over thirty minutes to pass one point.

Following the spectacle of the Grand United Procession, each society reverts to their own programme by holding their own Grand Procession. In these processions the societies bring out all the paraphernalia of their celebrations, banners, effigies, tableaux and tar barrels. Banners include large canvasses inscribed with mottoes and slogans including 'Good Old Cliffe', 'Hold them up Commercial', and the Bonfire Boys' Arms 'True to Each Other', while others portray the capture of Guy Fawkes and the burning of the Lewes Martyrs. The 'dummy' effigies, carried aloft with great ceremony, are replicas of the effigies of Guy Fawkes and Pope Paul V that are stuffed full of fireworks ready to be ignited during the firework display. Blazing tar barrels are dragged on iron trolleys through the streets to the firesites. Some societies, notably Cliffe, pull their tableau, a twice life-size three-dimensional model packed full of fireworks depicting a topical political topic, in the procession on a four wheeled wagon, or 'tab cart'.

The societies' Grand Processions progress through the town to their own firesites in fields on the town's outskirts. Here large fires have been burning long before the arrival of the processionists who are now joined by thousands of spectators gathered to watch the acting out of the time honoured firesite rituals. Four or five members, dressed in mock clerical regalia and resplendent in the names of 'Archbishop of the Cliffe' or 'Archbishop of St Johns' deliver speeches to the awaiting crowd denouncing unpopular politicians, enemies of Britain and opponents of

Mock 'clerics' delivering their annual oration to the crowd gathered at the firesite. The 'Archbishop' is flanked by his attendant clergy. (Photo: Pete Varnham)

Around midnight, Bonfire Boys and Girls jump through the fire of discarded torches at Cliffe Corner, the site of the original pre-1906 street bonfire. (Photo: Leigh Simpson)

the celebrations. Until recently the 'clergy' were the target for showers of fireworks and 'bangers', but as the availability of such rockets has declined so too has the practice. Following the speeches the effigies are condemned before being ignited followed by the tableau and associated aerial display which together form each society's magnificent firework display.

For the Bonfire Boys the remainder of the evening becomes a more private affair. For many it is the culmination of a year's work preparing for the celebrations and once the grand processions and firesite displays are successfully concluded and the crowds previously thronging the streets have drifted away the final processions become an opportunity for the members to relax, enjoy a few beers and generally 'let their hair down'. As midnight nears the Bonfire Boys can be seen dancing in the middle of the streets around the fires of discarded torches. But here, as during the rest of the evening, tradition is observed, the fires being placed on the societies' original pre-1906 firesites when street fires were permitted. The dancing and singing is not totally disorderly. 'Rule Britannia', 'God Save the Queen' and 'Auld Lang Syne' are sung in rotation until, shortly after midnight, the fire brigade arrives to douse the fires and the Bonfire Boys slowly disperse.

Other towns and villages in Sussex hold similar, if far less elaborate Guy Fawkes Night celebrations on Saturdays preceding and following the 'Fifth'. During the nineteenth century large celebrations were annually held in many more places throughout Southern England, but as these gradually declined or were suppressed Sussex, and in particular Lewes, became the acknowledged heart of 'Bonfire' where the celebrations witnessed today have survived largely unchanged for well over a century.

But why has Lewes maintained this annual commemoration of the Discovery of the Gunpowder Plot with so much ritual and pageantry? Before attempting to answer this question it is first necessary to understand the historical context in which the Plot occurred and the continuing religious tensions that arose in part from its discovery. Second there is a need to be aware of the political and religious conflicts within the small market town of Lewes that stimulated both support and opposition to the celebrations during the nineteenth century. Finally it is important to appreciate the inner dynamic sustaining the celebrations, the Bonfire Boys themselves and their desire to maintain what they consider to be the traditions of the 'Fifth'.

2. THE GUNPOWDER PLOT

At two o'clock on the morning of 5th November, 1605, Guy Fawkes was arrested in a vault beneath the House of Lords while guarding thirty-six barrels of gunpowder hidden under faggots of wood. A member of a group of Catholic conspirators led by Robert Catesby, it was Fawkes' task to light the fuse that would destroy the Parliament killing King James I and all those gathered for its opening. In the ensuing chaos a Catholic uprising led by Sir Edmund Digby was to seize the organs of power and install a Catholic monarch.

As a result of a letter sent by one of the conspirators, Francis Tresham, to his brother-in-law, the Catholic nobleman Lord Mounteagle, warning him not to attend the opening the Gunpowder Plot was discovered. Fawkes was imprisoned in the Tower while the other conspirators made good their escape from London to be later surrounded at Holbeach House on the borders of Staffordshire. Here Catesby and three fellow conspirators were slain, seven more being captured at Holbeach or elsewhere and returned to London. Guy Fawkes and his accomplices were tortured, tried and finally executed at the west end of St Paul's Churchyard on 30th and 31st January 1606, having confessed to their part in the plot.

Controversy now centres on the extent to which Robert Cecil, the chief minister, had prior knowledge of the Gunpowder Plot. Some argue that through the efficient operations of the secret police the Government was aware of the conspiracy long before Mounteagle revealed the contents of his letter. Allowing the plot to run

"The Great Conspiracy": a contemporary Dutch engraving of Guy Fawkes and his fellow conspirators.

12

its full course short of the final act provided Cecil with a propaganda coup of sufficient magnitude to totally discredit the Roman Catholics. Certainly the Government of James reacted swiftly and punitively against the co-religionists of Fawkes, two Acts being passed imposing restrictions and exclusions on Roman Catholics that separated them from other Englishmen.

The outburst of anti-Catholicism that followed the Plot was also given legal expression by the passing of a third Act entitled 'An Acte for a publique Thancksgiving to Almighty God everie yeere of the Fifte day of November' in January 1606. The Act proclaimed that the discovery of the plot should 'be held in a perpetual Remembrance' and that the 5th November be 'a holiday for ever in thankfulness to God for the deliverance and detestation of the Papists'. This annual 'remembrance' was to be in the form of a morning service in every parish church at which a special prayer of thanksgiving was to be offered up, bells rung and garrison canons fired. In the popular mind patriotism and anti-catholicism were inextricably intertwined. The Papacy was perceived as an alien political and religious power seeking to impose its dominion over Protestant England and by passing this Act the Government exploited such fears.

The romanticised image of Guy Fawkes preparing the fuse in readiness.

3. THE RIOTOUS YEARS, THE PRE-1847 CELEBRATIONS

The population of Lewes, in common with the rest of their Protestant countrymen undoubtedly observed the requirements of this Act, but it was not until 1679 that any elaborate celebrations were observed in the town. On 5th November of that year Benjamin Harris, writing in the Domestick Intelligence, reported a procession 'not unworthy taking notice of.' He describes how a company of young men armed with swords, muskets and pikes preceded several pictures, carried upon long poles, one representing a Jesuit with a bloody sword and a pistol, and inscribed: 'Our Religion is Murder, Rapine and Rebellion". Then came Guy Faux 'with his dark Lanthorn, being booted and spurred after the Old Fashion' followed by the Pope with his Cross Keys, Crosier, Staffe and other Fopperies, having his train borne up by several of his clergy.' There followed 'between twenty and thirty boys with vizards . . . one whereof carried Holy Water in a tin pot, sprinkling the people with a bottle-brush. In this manner they having carried his Holiness through the Town . . . they first degraded him, then committed him to the flames.' However it seems likely this and similar larger celebrations in London were provoked by the revelations of Titus Oates who, during 1679, falsely claimed the existence of a Popish Plot. The readiness to believe Oates' accusations reflected the continuing paranoiac fear of Roman Catholicism.

Little is known of the celebrations in 18th century Lewes. An entry in a church warden's account book of 1723 records payment for bell ringing on the 'Fifth' and in 1757 the town authorities paid two shillings for 'giving notice about the Bonfire and watching the same'. It is not until the early 1770s that the local press begins to describe in more detail the manner in which the 'custom' was carried out. Street bonfires, squibbing and a general disorder were common practice with an established firesite at the top of School Hill being the annual rendezvous for the Bonfire Boys. By 1785 the disturbances surrounding the celebrations were causing sufficient concern for the Riot Act to be read, nine ringleaders subsequently being sent to the House of Correction.

Attempts by the authorities to suppress the celebrations were met with determined opposition. In 1797 the Bonfire Boys, being threatened with stout opposition, were somewhat more than ordinarily ceremonious in the lighting of the bonfire. The man appointed to that post, with a dark lantern in one hand, a match in the other, and a bundle of shavings hung across his shoulder, and singing "God Save the King" proceeded to light the bonfire. However, following a particularly riotous 'Fifth' in 1806 during which eighteen Bonfire Boys were arrested, the bonfire was removed to the safety of Castle Banks on the outskirts of the town. Subsequently the celebrations went into decline and by 1814 the press was commenting that 'we scarcely remember our streets to have been so free from the annoyance of squibs, rockets and other fireworks'.

The celebrations enjoyed a resurgence during the 1820s and from this time were held each 5th November until 1913, except in 1874 when they were postponed until 30th December due to an outbreak of typhoid in the town. In 1821 the Sussex Weekly Advertiser noted that 'the excess of fireworks set off here on the last Monday evening reminded us of former times', this new-found enthusiasm manifesting itself two years later when the Bonfire Boys rekindled their defiance of the law by returning from Castle Banks to the High Street outside the Star Inn (now the Town Hall). Although printed notices were distributed by the constables prohibiting, on pain of imprisonment, the throwing of squibs there was a profusion of squibbing. In the absence of street bonfires squibbing continued as the principal entertainment for the Bonfire Boys throughout the 1820s.

In 1832 an innovation was introduced, blazing tar barrels being rolled through the streets. Opposition to this development made little impression on the Bonfire Boys who by 1834 were using the barrels to build a bonfire in the High Street outside County Hall (now the Law Courts). The rolling of tar barrels down School Hill became a sport, Bonfire Boys forming 'barrel parties' to drag the offending items about the town while the police attempted to arrest them or seize the 'tub'. Giving evidence before Magistrates in 1841 Superintendent Fagan, the officer in charge of the small Lewes Constabulary, described how he had observed about twenty persons dragging a barrel down the High Street to Friars Walk followed by 200 men, some of them of respectable appearance, but others in disguise.

The wearing of disguise which was evolving at this time was intended to avoid recognition and thus elude arrest. The police were instructed to arrest only those they did not recognise. Those they did 'had information lodged against them' and were arrested and charged later when confrontation or attack was less likely. Those wearing disguise who avoided immediate arrest thus escaped. The Bonfire Boys' disguises were initially of a rudimentary nature, people being observed with blackened faces and their coats turned inside out, but by 1847 one disguise foreshadowed what was to come. A man named Wimhurst, when arrested was dressed in a Guernsey shirt, a black leather belt with stars and over his face a white cap with holes cut for his eyes and mouth.

The Bonfire Boys who gathered annually in the High Street between County Hall and the Crown Hotel exhibited little respect for authority. Town officials, special constables, police and local magistrates were frequently assaulted while attempting to restrict the more extreme excesses perpetrated by the revellers. In 1841 police officers were set upon 'with force and arms to wit sticks stones bludgeons and other offensive weapons', Superintendent Fagan being 'struck on his head with a boulder, knocked down with bludgeons, and trampled upon.'

Violence often occurred when the authorities took action to restrict the Bonfire Boys' activities, a correspondent in the Advertiser commenting in 1841 that 'there was considerable greater tumult than has been experienced here for some years (due) to the rumoured concentration of the whole of the Constabulary Force in this place'. This belief undoubtedly contributed to the policy of non-intervention frequently pursued by the High Constables of the town, it usually being their practice to remain at County Hall and call upon the assistance of the police only if it really became necessary. Such inactivity was no doubt also influenced by insufficient force being available. The East Sussex Constabulary was not established until 1840 and then only one sergeant and three constables were stationed in Lewes. Prior to this law enforcement was the responsibility of local inhabitants, the magistrates swearing them in as special constables to police the celebrations.

The celebrations however did not meet with unanimous opposition. They were rowdy and dangerous, but little of serious consequence occurred. Windows were broken, but no houses were fired or destroyed. Assaults were perpetrated, but rarely resulted in serious injury. The celebrations, perceived as riotous by some, did not constitute a real threat to social order. Mr Creasy, the defence solicitor at the Assize Court following the 1847 disturbances no doubt spoke for many when he claimed that the celebrations were 'not what is ordinarily termed a riot, but was the keeping up of an old custom and might be regarded more as a frolic'. William Baxter, the proprietor of the Sussex Agricultural Express endorsed such sentiments in his editorial when he remarked that 'so long as the parties do no harm, there perhaps is no serious objection to our local act lying in abeyance for a few hours'. This was the prevailing opinion in 1846 when a policy of non-intervention was again adopted, Captain Mackay, the Chief Constable, being instructed not to interfere by the Lewes Bench of Magistrates, who had in turn received a written request to the same effect from the town's High Constables, Benjamin Flint and John Hilton.

The consequence of this inactivity was ultimately to lead to a transformation of the whole character of the Lewes celebrations. Following the building of a bonfire outside of County Hall the crowd, according to the Advertiser, 'emboldened by the impunity with which their outrages on the peace and respectability of the town had passed, the tar barrel party, who were disguised and who appeared to be under the management of some leader, and excited by drink and the riot of the whole scene, repaired about ten o'clock to the house of Mr Blackman, who, as an active and conscientious magistrate was well known to be opposed to the lawless proceedings of the bonfire rioters'. Here the Boys built a large bonfire of tar barrels, but when 'Mr Blackman, alarmed for the safety of his property, and to allay the fears of his company, went out and mildly, but firmly, desired the mob to disperse' he was met with 'derisive jeers, and fresh means were used to increase the flames.' On attempting 'to take one of the ringleaders into custody, which, when he had nearly accomplished, he received a blow over the eye from one of the numerous bludgeons which were on the instant raised, and was felled to the ground. Mr Blackman was picked up and carried into the house in a state of insensibility.' This incident had no effect on the mob, who for some hours afterwards continued their sport'.

Reaction to the assault on this elderly magistrate was immediate. George Bacon and W. E. Baxter through the editorials of their respective newspapers, the 'Advertiser' and 'Express' both condemned the Bonfire Boys' actions. An anonymous pamphlet written by 'An Old Inhabitant', but subsequently attributed to a local

school master, Mark Anthony Lower, was circulated. The author called for action to be taken to rid 'the town of Lewes of this abominable and disgraceful nuisance'. This call for the suppression of the celebrations was endorsed by Bacon, but Baxter in more conciliatory tone suggested the removal of the nuisance from the streets to a more suitable spot. He continued, 'We by no means agree with those who, from political motives, would put down the "Guys"'. Political and moral considerations appear to have been influencing attitudes towards the celebrations at this time. The Express, which supported the town's Conservative faction, consistently supported the celebrations frequently referring to the participants as patriotic, loyal citizens. The Advertiser, the clarion for the Liberal cause, conversely remained vehemently opposed to the celebrations, condemning them as 'riotous and brutalising orgies celebrated by a class of men taken from amongst the lowest ranks of society'.

Discussions at the January Quarter Sessions in 1847 signified the magistrates' determination to prevent disturbances occurring on the 'Fifth'. With the intention of reinforcing the magistrates' resolve a petition signed by thirty-two leading inhabitants of Lewes including wealthy merchants, solicitors, bankers and schoolmasters was presented to the Lewes Bench of Magistrates early in September. It called upon the magistrates to adopt measures sufficient to suppress the celebrations. The majority of the petitioners were High Street residents and consequently in most immediate danger from fire and the riotous proceedings, but more significantly they formed an influential social and political clique active in the town. Many were connected through marriage, business partnerships and political allegiance, all but three being Liberal supporters. Well over half also attended the various nonconformist chapels in the town.

The dominant body of opinion had previously persuaded the authorities from taking decisive action but the assault on Blackman enabled those opposed to the celebrations to gain the ascendency.

The prominent Liberal supporter and Tabernacle member, Mark Anthony Lower, was a vehement opponent of the Bonfire Boys. A signatory to the petition in 1847 the authorship of the anonymously published pamphlet circulated following the assault on Blackman has also been attributed to him.

Early in October a notice was issued by the Clerk of the Lewes Petty Sessions warning the Bonfire Boys of the magistrates' intentions.

At the Sessions on the 18th October it was reported that following discussions with the Secretary of State a body of London police would be made available to support the local constables. On 2nd November, following initial reluctance, 170 local tradesmen and gentry were sworn in as special constables in support of the regular police and troops. According to the Brighton Gazette two troops of Lancers at Brighton were kept under arms in readiness at a minute's notice if required.

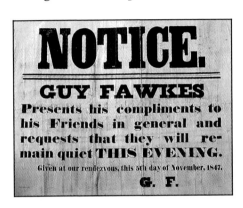

A leaflet distributed on 5th November 1847. Its sardonic tone well expresses the Bonfire Boys' attitude towards the action being taken against them by the authorities.

Thus the scene was set for confrontation. In the early hours of the 'Fifth' the local constables arrested eight men who were attempting to drag a lighted tar barrel down St Anne's Hill towards the High Street. At noon eighty London Police arrived and at four o'clock the special constables mustered at County Hall to receive their instructions. By eight o'clock a large crowd had assembled outside County Hall. Following the Brighton Mail coach horse taking fright at a squib the magistrates determined to act, Lord Chichester reading the Riot Act from the steps of County Hall before giving the crowd five minutes to disperse. Those Bonfire Boys who remained were driven from the High Street by the police. At twelve o'clock the specials were sent home and on Saturday morning the London Police departed by train, the aspect of the town being such as to induce the magistrates to think no further attempt would be made to break the peace.

But the magistrates misjudged the determination of the Bonfire Boys to resist. In the absence of law enforcers the town became the scene of nightly disturbances for the rest of the month. Crowds, often numbering more than a hundred, congregated in the High Street throwing fireworks and dragging tar barrels. The offices of the Advertiser were attacked as too was the Cliffe High Street residence of William Button, another leading Liberal opponent of the celebrations. It was not until special constables were again sworn in and extra police arrived that the rioting was finally suppressed.

The courts dealt severely with the sixteen men arrested during the disturbances.

The defendants secured sufficient financial assistance to employ the services of Mr Bennett, a Brighton solicitor, but he was unable to prevent eight defendants being sent to Assize where two were sentenced to six months hard labour, the others each to one month imprisonment. In his summing up Lord Denman indicated his belief that 'persons in a superior station of life were absurd and stupid enough to employ these poor people in this way, to annoy a class of persons who did not agree with them', hinting that the Conservatives had used the celebrations as a vehicle to wreak revenge on their Liberal opponents. Locally the July General Election had been particularly acrimonious, the sitting Conservative M.P. for Lewes, Sir Henry Fitzroy, having defected to the Peelites, joined the Liberal candidate, Robert Perfect, to defeat their Conservative opponents.

The Bonfire Boys had always enjoyed the support of wealthy and influential local Conservatives, much to the chagrin of their Liberal critics and it was leading Conservatives who promoted the compromise following the 1847 disturbances. The Constables of the Borough, Smart and Neal, approached the magistrates requesting that the town be left in their charge while a committee of local tradesmen chaired by Benjamin Flint, a local Conservative tea dealer, was formed to make the necessary preparations. They were assisted by two Lewes magistrates, John Ellman who supplied the field for the firesite and Sir Henry Shiffner who contributed the faggots for the bonfire. A subscription raised by the Constables was willingly and generously contributed to by several gentlemen of the town. At about seven o'clock on the evening of the 5th November 1848 a crowd of two thousand was enticed by a band away from the High Street to the firesite in Wallands Park where they harmlessly amused themselves. Judged a success, similar arrangements were carried through the following year.

4. ESTABLISHING A TRADITION, 1848-1903

The 'Fifth' had previously presented local young artisans, craftsmen and labourers with an opportunity to indulge in an evening's licence and to express their patriotic ardour and anti-Catholic sentiments. Ironically it was the actions of Pope Pius IX that enabled the Bonfire Boys to regain the initiative and return to the High Street. On 29th September, 1850, a Papal Bull proclaimed the restoration of the Catholic hierarchy in England, Cardinal Wiseman being created Archbishop of Westminster. The ensuing controversy provoked by this act of 'papal aggression' led to popular agitation throughout the country and in Lewes created a climate of toleration, if not open encouragement for the Bonfire Boys to rekindle the 'spirit of olden times'. They needed little encouragement to re-assert their customal 'rights'. In the Cliffe, barrels appeared in the streets and by seven o'clock a fire was kindled at Cliffe Corner. In the High Street a fire was lit outside County Hall and a crowd of three thousand gathered to hear an oration condemning Papal aggression delivered by a 'representation of "Cardinal Wiseman" dressed in red from top to toe'. But while the Bonfire Boys seized this opportunity they were aware of the need to curtail their riotous behaviour. Within three years this had been achieved, a form of celebrating the 'Fifth' being evolved that has remained largely unchanged through to the present day.

In 1853, at six o'clock, accompanied by a band, sixty to seventy Bonfire Boys

The 1853 Lewes Bonfire Society procession. Thomas Henwood, the artist of the painting from which this print was copied was living in Lewes at the time thus it is likely to be a fair representation of the scenes in Lewes High Street during the 1850s.

representing the Town Bonfire Society and dressed uniformly in Guernseys marched three or four abreast through the High Street, down St Mary's Lane and into Southover. At seven o'clock, from the top of Southover, the Grand Procession passed down Southover High Street, up St Mary's Lane and into the High Street where the fire was established in front of County Hall. Between half-past nine and ten o'clock the Grand Procession of the evening left the Pelham Arms and approached the fire. The band was followed by a large banner bearing the inscription 'NO POPERY'. It progressed down School Hill, into Albion Street, up East Street, into Market Street and back into the High Street to the fire. Here the crowd was addressed by a man in 'full canonicals'. An effigy of the Pope was suspended over the fire, followed by the Emperor of Russia. The crowd then flocked to Mount Pleasant where a firework display was held. At midnight the High Constable and Headboroughs announced that the celebration was at an end and the fire was extinguished. Similar proceedings were organised in Cliffe by the Cliffe Bonfire Society.

It remains unclear whether the initial 1848 committee chaired by Flint formed the 'Town' but by 1853 both it and the 'Cliffe' were organising separate celebrations

The Commercial Square Bonfire Society Staff in 1879. The seated figure resplendent in clerical attire is Lewis Miles, the 'Archbishop of St Johns-sub-Castro'. To his right in cocked hat is Ernest Trayton Hall, the Society's Commander-in-Chief, and to his left the Society's secretary, William Alfred Pollard. Miles was the son of a High Street grocer, Hall a newspaper reporter and High Street tobacconist and Pollard a solicitor's general clerk living in East Street. In 1879 they were aged 20, 24 and 23 respectively.

A modern counter-part of the nineteenth century barrel runs has in recent years been recreated by the Cliffe Society, members racing their 'barrels' from Cliffe Bridge to Cliffe Corner before the commencement of the processions. (Photo: Leigh Simpson)

in their respective areas of Lewes. By 1857 the Commercial Square Bonfire Society had been formed and the 'Town' had changed its name to the 'Lewes', later known as the Lewes Borough Bonfire Society. These three societies were joined by Southover Bonfire Society in 1886 and while two other societies were formed during this period, 'Waterloo' and 'St Anne's', they were in existence for only short periods, Waterloo between 1857-58 and 1876-80 and St Anne's from 1876 to 1880.

Who formed the bonfire societies remains unclear. Tom Jenner, a local butcher, is reputed to have been a founding member of Commercial Square and two local brewers, Thomas Monk and Francis Verrall, were leading Borough figures in the early 1850s. Much later Tom Wheeler, a resident of South Street, formed the South Street Juvenile Bonfire Society in 1913 for the children living in the Cliffe area. Indeed the early committees appear to have been shrouded in secrecy, the identity of their members being closely guarded. In a letter dated December 1881 the Chief Constable, Captain Mackay, felt obliged to deny receiving information regarding the identity of the Borough committee from a waiter at the Brewer's Arms.

Each society celebrated the 'Fifth' in a similar way, their activities becoming more organised and elaborate as the century progressed. A typical 'Fifth' was ushered in by a 'salvo of artillery' from Cliffe Hill at midnight, the singing of 'Rule Britannia', the 'National Anthem', and the reciting of the 'Bonfire Prayers' outside County Hall. During the course of the day effigies of Guy Fawkes were paraded from pub to pub by groups of youths and by four o'clock people whose houses were along the processional routes were taking the usual precautions against fire by barricading the lower windows and covering their cellar gratings with wet straw. Not long after, special trains from Brighton, Eastbourne, Uckfield and other places, including London, began arriving bringing visitors to swell the crowds of local spectators. Meanwhile costumed members of the various societies were making their way to their respective headquarters at local public houses in readiness for the first processions.

Before the processions commenced each society ran their barrels through the streets prior to pitching them at their firesites. The 'runs' went from their headquarters to designated points, returning to their firesite where the remains of the barrels were pitched to form the bonfire. The Borough's 'run' went from the Pelham Arms to County Hall via Cliffe Bridge, Cliffe from either South Street or Malling Street via Cliffe Bridge to Cliffe Corner and Southover from the King's Head to the Manor House in Southover High Street and back. Commercial Square pitched their fire in Commercial Square opposite the Police Station. For the remainder of the evening the fire became the focal point for the societies' activities.

Once the fires were established the first processions, taking a regimented order, marched through the town. In 1889, according to the Express, 'the Commander gave his order to his lieutenants, who passed it on to another, and so on, until there is a regular din, to which is added the continual reports of troublesome "rousers", which were by this time being discharged pretty freely. Eventually the order was given to "light up", and instantly numerous torches and coloured fire lit up the thoroughfare. The band struck up a popular air, and as the procession moved forward it was indeed a very picturesque sight. Half a dozen or more gaudily-attired Indians acted as pioneers, and behind these followed the staff, several wearing beautiful dresses, the Commander-in-Chief occupying a prominent centre position. He wore the dress of a hussar, which was very appropriate to his office. He was supported by a Court page, and jester as his lieutenants; a body of seven or eight Hungarian hussars formed his body guard. Then came the band, in front of which marched the captain, wielding his staff, and following the musicians were other members carrying torches and other lights. The whole was brought up by two sledges of tar barrels, which threw out tremendous heat and caused the spectators to draw back as they passed. Having processed a number of times around their locality the societies each converged on their firesite where the 'Bishop' gave his annual oration to the gathered crowd and the effigies and tableau were ignited and burnt. The evening was concluded by one more procession to use up the surplus torches, tubs, and other combustibles, followed by 'Bonfire Prayers' and "God Save the Queen", after which the Borough Fire Brigade extinguished the fires'.

In this way the bonfire societies transformed a night of riot into an organised and fairly disciplined street celebration. The most significant feature of this change was the introduction of torchlit processions of costume clad members carrying banners and accompanied by bands. Each society held as many as eight

THE ORDER OF PROCESSIONS,

Of the Lewes Bonfire Society, for the Sixth of November, 1854.

All to meet at the Pelham Arms, at six o'clock, precisely.

1.—To form a procession four abreast, with the Band, and start at half-past six, to go down the Town and St. Mary's lane, to the Swan Inn, Southover.

2.—The procession to start from the Swan Inn, Southover, quarter before seven, with the Band, Banners, 25 Torches, 2 large Tubs, and 4 small Tar Barrels.

3.—Four small Tubs and 12 Torches to start from the Pelham Arms at half-past seven, to proceed to the Bridge, one to be thrown into the river, the remainder to be brought back to the County Hall, and put on the fire.

4.—Three small Tubs at quarter-past eight, to proceed down Town, through Albion Street, back to the County Hall.

THE GRAND PROCESSION,

To start at nine o'clock.

CAPTAIN

Lieutenant   Lieutenant
Seven Lieutenants with Torches
Pope   Guy Fawkes
Bishop of Newtown
Banner No Popery
Band
One Hundred Torches
Banner Bonfire Boys Arms
Four large Tubs
(drawn by Harberds party)
Six small Tar Barrels
Banner God save the Queen

Small Banners   *Small Banners*

6.—Two large Tubs and 4 small ones to be lighted at the County Hall, and drawn to the Bridge, with Band, Banners, and thirteen Torches.

7.—Two small Barrels, down the Town, through Star Lane, down West Street, up Market Street to the County Hall.

8.—One large Tub and 2 small ones, to start from the Pelham Arms, to the County Hall, with Band, Banners, and the whole strength of the company singing, and the Band playing GOD SAVE THE QUEEN.

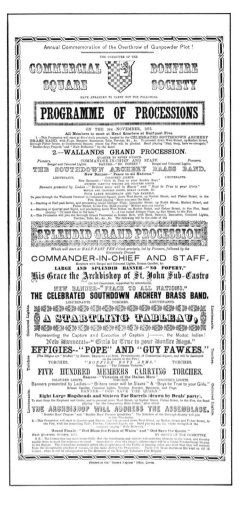

Programmes of the Lewes Bonfire Society in 1854 and the Commercial Square Bonfire Society in 1873. Each society published its own programme, but they were similar in format and content. A comparison illustrates how as the century progressed the arrangements became increasingly more elaborate.

processions between five o'clock and eleven o'clock, adhering to published timetables and processional routes. The purpose of the early processions was to drag blazing tar barrels through the streets, but the highlight of the evening's parades were the 'Grand' processions which preceded each society's firesite display. Effigies of the Pope, Guy Fawkes and other notorieties were paraded while the society's tableau, borne on a cart was drawn, often by horses, to the firesite. Such was the importance placed on this procession that it became the custom for societies to support each others 'Grand', Commercial Square annually marching from their

The Borough's 1872 Commander-in-Chief, George Lipscombe, accompanied by his 'valet', Edward Dowlen. George was the son of a High Street butcher, John Lipscombe, while Dowlen was employed as a butcher's assistant. The master-servant relationship was thus extended from the workplace to the Society hierarchy.

25

headquarters at the Elephant and Castle to Rotten Row to join the Borough's 'Grand'. By 1894 Commercial Square was in turn being supported by both Borough and Cliffe.

The processions were regimented and well marshalled, the societies appointing officers from among their own members to police the processions. Initially the officers entrusted with this task were referred to as 'Captains' but as the societies became more established the numbers and titles of officers became increasingly high-sounding. In 1899 the Commercial Square's processions were marshalled by a Commander-in-Chief, a Chief Pioneer, Staff Officers, Staff Marshal, Staff Bearer, 1st and 2nd Lieutenants, Grooms in Waiting, Chief of Staff, Staff Bugler, Field Marshals, Staff Surgeon, Aides de Camp, Inspector General, Ambulance Staff, Yeoman of the Tableau, Captain of Ranks, and Lieutenants of Ranks.

Initially officers were identified by their insignia of office, in 1853 the wearing of red sashes. As their numbers increased and fancy dress began to replace the uniform guernsey, officers were more frequently seen wearing elaborate costumes which distinguished them from other processionists. Often their costumes complemented their military title emphasising a militarist characteristic often found among the Bonfire Boys. In 1880 the Borough's Commander-in-Chief wore a red frock coat, trimmed with gold, black nether garments with top boots, sash of gold and silk, and silver helmet and plume, the ordinary every-day garb of a general of the British Army.

The development of costumes among the officers reflected a trend away from

The Cliffe's pioneer front in 1913. Compared with the spectacular and expensive homemade costumes worn by today's Bonfire Boys and Girls these 'Roman guards' are rudimentary. Immediately after the First World War pioneer costumes were hired from theatrical costumiers, perhaps in an effort to improve the quality of fancy dress worn in the processions.

costumes being worn as a disguise towards fancy dress intended to impress the spectators. In 1852 the 'Town' Bonfire Boys adopted the 'Guernsey', a black and white striped jersey, and white trousers while those in Cliffe appeared in 'white frocks outside red inexpressibles'. By 1859 costumes included Greek warriors and Chickasaw Indians. In the 1880s the Guernseys had all but disappeared, the processionists wearing a wide variety of costumes including 'devils, clowns, pantaloons, Salvation Army representatives, Shakers, cavaliers, sprites, jesters, courtiers, troubadours, tambourine girls in Italian costume, Zouaves, artillerymen, chasseurs, sailors and niggers'.

The variety of costumes resulted in a further structuring of the processions. Groups attired in the same costume and known as 'pioneers' led the processions under the direction of a Pioneer Chief. Often the pioneers had some contemporary relevance. In 1862 Cliffe, Borough and Commercial Square all had groups dressed 'in Garibaldian costume, red shirt, white trousers, and top boots'. Zulu and soldiers were worn at the time of the Zulu Wars in 1879, and a squad of Lancers reflected England's Sudanese campaign in 1897. Other pioneer costumes were chosen for more ephemeral reasons, red indians being particularly popular with both Commercial Square and Borough.

The regimentation of the processions was aided by the use of bands. First introduced during the 1840s, bands accompanied processions and supplied specific musical items at different stages during the evening's events. 'Slap, bang, here we are again' always announced the societies' first processions followed by 'See the Conquering Hero Come', played during their Grand processions. 'Rule Britannia' accompanied the burning of the effigies of Guy Fawkes and the Pope while the proceedings of all the societies were concluded with the playing of the 'National Anthem'. The names of the bands suggest that the musical accompaniment was of good quality. In 1858 the Brighton Town Band and the Lewes Saxhorn Band accompanied the Cliffe and Commercial Square respectively and in 1862 Borough were joined by the Brighton Rifle Corp Band. A humorous note was introduced in 1895 when the Borough's band was referred to as the 'Society's specially trained original fire-proof band'.

Initially the purpose of the processions was to provide parties of Bonfire Boys the opportunity to continue to drag burning tar barrels through the streets. The importance of barrels however declined as the century progressed, their numbers diminishing as they began to be drawn on sledges, but they retained a symbolic significance. It became the practice of each society to throw a single burning barrel from Cliffe Bridge into the River Ouse, a practice first recorded, without explanation, in 1855. By 1874 it had become associated with the exchange of fraternal greetings on the bridge between 'Cliffe' and 'Borough' in recognition of the bridge marking the territorial boundary between the two societies. First mentioned in 1857 this encounter was colourfully described by the Express when it noted that 'Gentlemen from the classic district of Toby's Town and the purlieus of St John's affectionately greeted and warmly shook hands with gentlemen from the quiet secluded retreat of Swing Pump, and many a foaming cup was crushed in drinking the pledge that "Britons never shall be slaves" '. Fraternal greetings are no longer exchanged, but the societies continue to throw a blazing tar barrel into the Ouse each year.

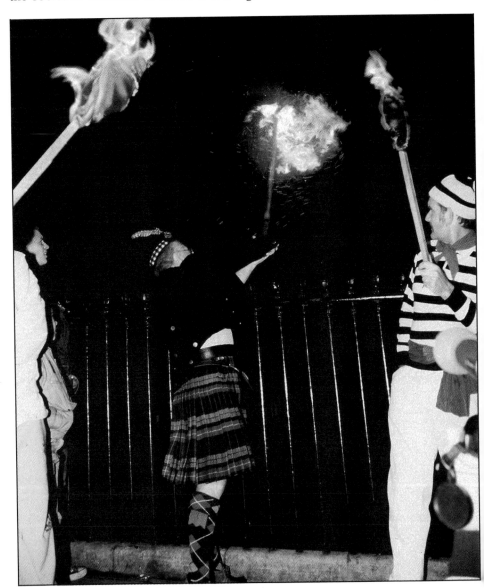

All the bonfire societies throw a blazing tar barrel from Cliffe Bridge into the River Ouse during the early part of the evening. Here Aubrey Taylor performs the ritual which he has done for the Cliffe Society since 1945. (Photo: Phil Everitt)

5. RELIGION, POLITICS AND FIREWORKS

It was at the firesite that the Bonfire Boys expressed their religious and political allegiances. While 'No Popery' banners were carried in the processions it was through the speeches of the mock clerics, the effigies and the tableaux that the Bonfire Boys' anti-Catholicism was expressed. Resplendent in such grandiose titles as 'Bishop of Newtown', 'The Lord Bishop of the Cliffe', or 'His Grace the Archbishop of St John-sub-Castro' the mock clerics became the official mouth-piece of their societies. It was their appointed task to harangue the crowd before condemning the effigies to the fire. Throughout the nineteenth century their speeches took on a strong anti-Catholic tone, the Papacy continuing to be perceived as a threat to Protestant Britain. In a typical firesite speech in 1874 the 'Bishop of Cliffe' forcefully expressed the opinion that 'what the Catholics aspire to is universal dominion all over the world, with the Pope at their head.' He continued, 'We must remember that they are now what they always were in ancient times, and had they the power they would put an end to Protestantism'.

Such attitudes were given symbolic representation by the annual burning of the effigy of the Pope in the company of the conspirator Guy Fawkes. In 1851 the effigies of the Pope and Wiseman were paraded around the town before being burnt on the fire outside County Hall, but in the following year the Pope suffered this fate alone. In the period leading up to 1913 the effigies of Pius IX, whose pontificate lasted from 1846 to 1878, and that of his successor Leo XIII were burnt. The Bonfire Boys were frequently criticised by Catholics and more tolerant Protestants for this expression of religious bigotry and such was the controversy aroused by Pope burning that the matter was raised in the House of Commons in 1902 by Mr J. Tully, member for South Leitrim, when he asked the Secretary of State for the Home Department whether he was aware of the occurrences in Lewes. Either in response to such criticism or because of a change in attitude the Commercial Square in 1893 burnt an effigy of Pope Paul V, the Pope at the time of the Gunpowder Plot. However the other societies continued to burn the offending effigy of the incumbent Pope.

As if to reinforce the religious character of the celebrations at this time a Thanksgiving Service was inaugurated by the Reverend Richardson at Southover Church in 1893. Held on the Sunday prior to the 'Fifth' the service was attended by members of all the societies. Ostensibly to give thanks to God for delivering England from the Gunpowder Plot the service became an opportunity to attack Popery. Richardson annually warned his congregation of the dangers to civil and religious liberties that accompanied any growth of Roman Catholicism while his successor, the Reverend Lee Elliott, emphasised that Protestantism was the raison d'etre of the service. The Thanksgiving Service was transferred to Jireh Chapel in 1905 where it has been held annually until the chapel's closure during the late 1980s.

Neither were the nineteenth century Bonfire Boys afraid of becoming embroiled in local religious controversy. In 1858 an effigy of 'Old Neale', representing the

Many tableaux took on an anti-Catholic theme during the Edwardian period in response to the influx into Britain of Catholics escaping the anti-clerical measures being taken by the French Government. Borough's 1903 tableau was entitled 'Returned with Thanks: the solution to the alien question especially as regards monastic orders'. Cliffe's 1910 tableau, 'Popery on the Rocks' (alternatively entitled 'Not Wanted, Evicted Monks') expressed similar sentiments while its 1913 tableau, 'The Popish Pedlar', alludes to door-to-door salesmen raising money for the Roman Catholic Church.

Reverend John Mason Neale accompanied Fawkes and the Pope. The founder of an Anglican sisterhood at St Margaret's in East Grinstead, Neale had during the previous November attempted to attend the funeral of one of his converts, Emily Scobell, the eldest daughter of the Reverend John Scobell, Rector of Southover and All Saints. Neale accompanied the coffin along with eight Sisters to Lewes, but their arrival aroused considerable excitement due to the semi-Papistical emblems that adorned the coffin. Shouts of 'No Popery' were heard and the crowd proceeded to manhandle Neale who was forced to seek refuge in the King's Head until the police could escort him back to the railway station. The subsequent acquittal of a man accused of throwing stones at Neale so delighted the crowd that the town band was brought out.

A few years later a catholic priest, the Reverend Drinkwater, moved into Priory Crescent to administer to Catholic prisoners held in Lewes Prison. His arrival provoked a spate of placards stuck around the town proclaiming 'No Popery — Protestants of Lewes, beware of the Crescent'. Passions were further roused when it was learnt he had set up a chapel in his home. Hostile crowds gathered outside his residence on Sunday evenings and in 1867 the Borough Society's procession stopped opposite Priory Crescent while an effigy of Drinkwater was exploded. For the succeeding two years the Pope's effigy was likewise ignited in front of his house.

The opening of the Roman Catholic Chapel on 25th January, 1870 caused a similar furore. The Bonfire Boys had

'The Way to Rome', the Cliffe Society's 1925 tableau. The Captains of Tableau responsible for its construction were Messrs. A. Eager (seated) and W. Fielder (second from left). St Michael's Church was always viewed with suspicion by the Bonfire Boys because of the High Church rituals performed there.

made their feelings known the previous 'Fifth', the Borough's tableau depicting a Romish priest, with bell, book, candle, and crucifix, in the act of laying the chapel's foundation stone. On the day the chapel opened a crowd approaching a thousand people was restrained from committing acts of violence by a strong police presence while a full muster of Bonfire Boys attending a meeting at their headquarters, the Pelham Arms, adjacent to the chapel were deterred from becoming involved by the intervention of the parish officials. As the congregation left the service a number of Protestants who had attended were jostled by the crowd. In the ensuing court case five men, including John Carey, the Borough's 'Bishop', were fined for their part in the disturbances. Summing up the Chairman of the Bench, Lord Chichester, instructed the licensee of the Pelham Arms not to permit Borough Society meetings to coincide with services at the chapel.

The introduction of Romanist practices into the Church of England similarly provoked the Bonfire Boys. Many, including local clergy and Protestant organisations attributed the success of the Catholics in Lewes to Puseyism. Well attended Protestant meetings were held in the town and the Anglo-Catholic church of St Michaels became the focus of the Bonfire Boys attention. In 1871 the 'Archbishop' of Commercial Square commented that a clergyman of a Protestant parish in Lewes was endeavouring to follow the practices which were

The Martyr's Memorial was unveiled by the Countess of Portsmouth on 8th May 1901. The controversy surrounding its erection was acknowledged by the 'Lord High Chancellor of Southover' during his firesite speech. He claimed it was not meant 'as a slap in the face to our fellow Roman Catholic townsmen but as a silent, yet speaking, witness for the truth'.

observed at the Roman Catholic Chapel. In 1877 the newly appointed Rector, E. H. Cross, was forced to resign his membership of two ritualistic societies, the English Church Union and the Society of the Holy Cross, following criticism in the town. On the 'Fifth' the Borough's tableau was entitled "Showing our disapproval of the attempt of the members of the Holy Cross Society to introduce the Confessional and the use of the Book called "The Priest in Absolution" in the Church of England". His successor, the Reverend Belcher, again attracted the attention of the Bonfire Boys during the late 1890s, but he was made of sterner stuff, continuing to champion his cause by writing on the subject of ritualism in the 'Church Times'. This reaction to what was perceived as Romanish practices at St Michael's continued after the First World War, the Cliffe Society's 1925 tableau entitled 'The Way to Rome' being a model of St Michael's Church.

The high point of Protestantism in Lewes occurred in 1901 when the Martyrs' Memorial (see page 32) dedicated to the seventeen Protestant martyrs who were burnt at the stake outside the Star Inn in the High Street between 1555 and 1557 was unveiled. Efforts to erect some form of monument were first made in 1889, but provoked considerable controversy, the Town Council declining to become involved. Opponents including a leading Quaker, Alderman Kemp, and the Reverend Belcher, vicar of St Michael's, claimed it would offend Roman Catholic inhabitants. The societies' clerics applauded the memorial's erection and from that date references began to be made to the Martyrs during the celebrations.

The Bonfire Boys support for the Monarchy, the Conservative Party and Imperialism were similar expressed through their banners, clerical speeches, effigies and tableaux. Their loyalty to the Monarchy was proclaimed on banners bearing inscriptions including 'God Save the Queen', 'Long May Victoria Live' and 'Protect our Queen and Constitution'. The Bonfire Boys were, and continue to be active in organising torchlight processions for commemorative celebrations in Lewes, many of them Royal occasions. The marriage of the Prince of Wales in 1863 was the first time the societies co-operated in this way and in 1893 the marriage of the Duke of York and Princess May of Teck was similarly celebrated. In 1887 and 1897 Queen Victoria's Silver and Diamond Jubilees were commemorated by torchlight processions followed by the Coronations of Edward VII in 1902 and George V in 1911.

British Imperialist adventures were also celebrated by the Bonfire Boys. Crimean victories and Indian successes were for a long time recorded on banners while the subject of effigies, tableaux and costumes similarly reflected these events. At the time of the Crimean War in 1855 the effigy of the Emperor of Russia was burnt. In 1857 attention was turned to India where mutineers were perpetrating atrocities on British troops and civilians, the Bonfire Boys responding by destroying effigies of the King of Bombay. The successful British military intervention in Afghanistan in 1878 was the topic of the firesite speech at Commercial Square while Afghan costumes were worn in Borough's procession and the Waterloo tableau depicted 'Britannia in the middle and in each corner the heads of the Ameer of Afghanistan, a Zulu king and the heads of two well known criminals'. In 1882 the defeat of

Arabi Pasha, the Egyptian nationalist, by British troops at Tel-el-Kebir was praised by the 'Bishops' of Borough and Commercial Square. The Borough's tableau, 'Arabi Pasha surrendering to the British General' glorified the British military success while generals' uniforms and Egyptian costumes were worn by Borough and Cliffe members. Support for the Boer War was also manifest through the tableaux of Borough, Cliffe and Commercial Square in 1899, entitled respectively 'Briton or Boer', 'Kruger Delivering His Last Speech from the Praeed Kraal' and 'The Wheel of Fortune and War'. Costumes worn during the war's duration were particularly militaristic, the Borough's 1899 pioneers being '17th Lancers in blue and New South Wales Lancers in khaki' while their band was aptly named 'The Kimberley Silver Saxophonists'.

Many of the leading Bonfire Boys at this time were also members of the town's thriving Conservative dominated Volunteer units. Private T. Jenner snr., a founding member of Commercial Square who chaired the Society's annual dinner for over thirty years served in the Volunteers for nearly 25 years while W. T. Gearing, a founding member of Borough retired as Colour Sergeant at the age of 55 after 33 years service. Following Gearing's retirement H. E. Philcox, a leading officer of the Cliffe Society was promoted to Colour Sergeant. Undoubtedly considering it their patriotic duty their support for the military was also annually proclaimed in toasts to the 'Army, Navy and Volunteers' at the societies' dinners and on banners proclaiming 'Army and Navy', 'Success to the Volunteers' and 'Our Army and Navy, may success ever attend them' carried in the processions.

The Bonfire Boys claimed to be non-political but they frequently criticised Liberal Governments for their reluctance to pursue a vigorous Imperial policy. In 1877 the Borough's 'Bishop' expressed his pleasure that England was under a Conservative Ministry and was thus not rushing into war in Bulgaria while a few years later he spoke out against the weaknesses of the past Liberal Government. In 1880, following the defeat of Disraeli's Government, Gladstone's withdrawal of troops from Afghanistan 'before the work they had been sent to perform was completed' was critically alluded to by the Borough's 'Bishop'. Gladstone's support for Irish Home Rule was likewise condemned, religious considerations colouring the rhetoric of the 'Bishops'.

The Bonfire Boys however reserved their political venom for Socialism. In 1887, Jubilee year, the Borough's 'Bishop' urged the spectators to disregard the clap-trap of Socialists and to remain loyal to the Queen. In 1894 the Scottish miners' strike was attributed to Socialist agitators and in September 1907, when the Brighton Councillor, W. Evans, attempted to hold a Socialist debate at the top of School Hill he was greeted by a rowdy crowd who taunted him with shouts of 'Burn him' and proceeded to drown his speech with the 'Bonfire Prayers' and the singing of 'Rule Britannia'.

While effigies and tableaux reflected the contemporary political and religious attitudes of the Bonfire Boys they also became the vehicle for their developing pyrotechnic artistry. Effigies were originally carried on poles and thrown onto the

Borough Society members posing in front of their 1905 tableau, 'Guy Fawkes Monument'. It is flanked by the effigies of the Pope and Guy Fawkes. In the foreground is an iron trolley bearing three tar barrels, later to be drawn in the procession. A similar trolley is still used for this purpose by the Cliffe Society.

bonfire, but while this remained the fate of Guy Fawkes and the Pope other individuals who provoked the wrath of the Bonfire Boys were dispensed with in an increasingly more audacious and imaginative manner with the use of fireworks and large three dimensional structures. In 1853 a representation of Peter Bacon in the form of a pig had been hurled onto the bonfire. The continuing opposition to the celebrations of the Advertiser's proprietor had so provoked the ire of the Bonfire Boys that according to Samuel Elphick, a corn merchant of Cliffe, in a letter to his brother in Australia 'the Boys sent him a parcel of potato peelings and cabbage leaves for his hog.' Seven years later this lampooning of popular notorieties had developed into the first tableau. An effigy of Thomas Hopley, a local school teacher who had been sentenced to four years imprisonment at Lewes Assizes for beating a pupil to death, met a similar fate to that of Bacon at the Borough's firesite. However his effigy was not carried on a pole but borne on a cart, dressed in a tight fitting suit, with a stick, apparently thrashing a lad borne on the same platform.

The theatrical nature of these early tableaux, the involvement of 'actors' and the apparent lack of fireworks is indicated by a description of Borough's 1864 tableau

The scene outside the White Hart Hotel on the 'Fifth', 1901. The Borough's tableau entitled 'Enemies of the Empire' depicts a Roman chariot drawn by two dapple greys with saddle cloths inscribed 'Treason' and 'Anarchy' and driven by 'Popery' in the guise of Old Nick. The 'Archbishop' is seen to the left addressing the crowd. (Photo: Edward Reeves)

Cliffe Corner in 1902. St Thomas a'Becket Church provides the backdrop for the Cliffe Society's tableau, 'The Eruption of Mount Pelee in the West Indies'. The clergy are delivering their speech from the second floor parapet of Bosher's shop. The Martyr's Memorial can be seen illuminated above the roofs of the buildings. (Photo: Edward Reeves)

entitled 'Franco-Italian Treaty'. It consisted of an enormous clerical figure with "Rome" on its breast accompanied by two individuals, one attired in a cocked hat, boots and a tasteful military uniform representing Napoleon, the other in a slouch hat, red shirt, and white trousers representing Garibaldi. The 'Bishop' explained that Napoleon was trying to hold possession of Rome against the effort of Garibaldi and that a desperate struggle would ensue in which Napoleon would be wounded, the Italian Liberator victorious, and the Papal tyrant hurled into the flames. A struggle did ensue, Napoleon and Garibaldi crossing swords a few times in melodramatic fashion before Napoleon fell, or rather, sat down.

However fireworks soon began to be incorporated and by the turn of the century the tableaux had become the central feature of the firework displays. In 1895 Borough's 24 feet high tableau representing a golden domed mosque was surmounted by a disc platform on which was seated the "Unspeakable Turk" smoking a chibouque. On the corners of the roof were four attendant imps, all in effigy. Following the 'Bishop's oration the disc on the platform on which "The Turk" was seated revolved amidst a blaze of fireworks, and a fountain of golden rain broke out over his head in the shape of a fiery umbrella. Coloured fires and Roman candles erupted all over the structure and finally the Turk was destroyed by mines called "Jack-in-box".

Borough introduced their first tableau in 1860, but it was not until 1869 that Cliffe appears to have introduced this innovation with a tableau containing the effigies of a Priest and a Nun, followed in 1873 by Commercial Square's first tableau entitled 'Capture and Execution of Capt Jack, the Modoc Indian'. Southover, although formed in 1886, did not introduce tableaux until 1897. Two local tradesmen, Harry Philcox, a watchmaker trading in Cliffe and Frederick Beeching, a baker living in West Street are attributed with the construction of many of these tableaux. Philcox was the Cliffe's 'tab' maker while Beeching, who was licensed to supply and manufacture fireworks, built both Commercial Square's and Borough's tableaux being succeeded by his sons James and John following his death in 1879.

Although the Bonfire Boys conducted the 'Fifth' in an orderly, if still lively way many Liberal non-conformists and supporters of the local Temperance movement continued to oppose the celebrations for moral and religious reasons. The survival of Bonfire Night in Lewes has been frequently attributed to the strength of nonconformity in the town, but the public display of excess in which the Bonfire Boys conducted themselves provoked steadfast condemnation if not active opposition from this quarter. The vast majority of Bonfire Boys and their wealthy supporters were Anglican and not members of the town's numerous nonconformist sects. Rather than being an expression of nonconformity the Bonfire Boys' anti-Catholic stance is rooted in the 'Church and King' tradition of popular Protestantism, in which the Church of England was seen as the national church and a bulwark against the political and religious aspirations of the Papacy.

6. CHANGE IMPOSED, 1904-1913

Within this scenario it is not surprising that as in 1846, a single incident provided the opportunity for these critics to mobilize sufficient opposition to impose changes on the celebrations. During the early hours of Tuesday 4th October, 1904, only one month before the 'Fifth', smoke was observed coming from the premises of Dusart's shop at 85 High Street. The local fire appliance proved totally inadequate and by the time the Brighton Fire Brigade arrived at mid-day the building had been razed to the ground, the adjoining properties only being saved due to their brick construction.

Dusart's shop before and after the disastrous fire that razed the premises to the ground. It was fortunate that the buildings on either side were constructed of brick, thus preventing the fire from spreading along the timber-frames of the majority of High Street properties.

The societies responded by issuing notices condemning the use of the notorious homemade squib, the 'Lewes Rouser', and restricting the size of their tar barrels, but despite this Borough suffered a marked decline in financial support. The 1904 celebrations were uneventful, but during 1905 a petition was circulated calling for the suppression of the celebrations. Signed by 94 inhabitants including, it was claimed, ten magistrates, the petition was submitted to the Joint Standing Committee of the East Sussex County Council in October, but on the advice of the Chief Constable the Committee deferred consideration until the following year.

The petition provoked hostility from the outset. Its instigators drew attention to the danger of fire arising from the celebration, but their ulterior motives soon became apparent. The petitioners further antagonised local feeling by submitting their petition directly to the County Council, by-passing the Borough Council. This action was undoubtedly influenced by the petitioners' concern regarding the partiality of the Town Council, many councillors including the then Mayor, John Miles, being supporters of the celebrations. Others, including Joseph Hardwick and Percy King, were members of the societies, King having been chairman of Commercial Square since 1894.

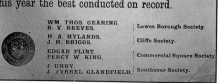

Two notices issued by the Amalgamated Bonfire Societies of Lewes in response to the fears arising from Dusart's fire. Spectators are requested not to let off Lewes Rousers and Large Roman Candles, but the societies did not modify their own activities.

To counter this threat the bonfire societies co-ordinated their response, a joint meeting being held on 12th October at the Royal Oak attended by representatives from the four societies. A counter-petition, signed by 492 inhabitants of Lewes and 287 persons from surrounding villages requesting that no action should be taken against the celebrations was subsequently submitted to the Joint Standing Committee. At their quarterly meeting on 23rd January, 1906 the Committee set up a sub-committee to deal with the matter, the sub-committee inviting representatives of both parties to speak in support of their respective petitions.

The wording of the original petition indicated that fear of fire was not the petitioners only concern. While calling for the suppression of bonfires and explosives in the streets they also requested greater activity in the arrest of drunken persons, claiming that the law was openly and flagrantly broken. According to the petitioners the 'Fifth' was an occasion for immorality and drunkenness. Certainly drunken behaviour had always been an element of the celebrations, it being frequently observed that among those taking part many were intoxicated. The connection between the Bonfire Boys and beer was well established, public houses being used by the bonfire societies for their headquarters and venues for committee meetings, annual dinners and social gatherings. As a consequence support for the bonfire societies from the licensed victuallers and the brewing interest was considerable.

The last bonfire and firework display in Lewes High Street, Monday 6th November 1905. In the background the Borough's tableau, 'Guy Fawkes Monument' is exploding while the 'Archbishop', William Gearing delivers his annual oration. (Photo: Edward Reeves)

...litical protagonists take issue over the celebrations. The Conservative George Holman (left) upholds ...dition and the 'rights' of the Bonfire Boys while his Liberal adversary, Caleb Rickman Kemp (right), ...ls for their suppression.
(Photo: Edward Reeves)

Addressing his congregation in 1879, the Reverend Armstrong of Eastgate Baptist ...urch had lamented the drunkenness, profane language and carnal sin associated ...th the celebrations. Such opposition was echoed in statements before the sub-...mmittee. A leading spokesman for the petitioners, Caleb Rickman Kemp, an ...luent Liberal businessman, influential Quaker, Lewes Mayor and County ...uncillor, who was also actively involved in the town's flourishing temperance ...ovement raised just this issue. Two other Lewes clergymen, Reverend Duncan-...arce, Rector of St Anne's and Reverend John Penfold Morris of East Gate Baptist ...urch endorsed Kemp's accusation. All three were associated with the local branch ...the British Womens' Temperance Association while Band of Hope meetings ...re regularly held at the Baptist Church. A fourth clergyman, the Reverend R. ...Belcher of St Michael's also spoke before the subcommittee on behalf of the ...titioners. He had already provoked the wrath of the Bonfire Boys for his 'Romanist' ...idencies and was no doubt motivated on this occasion more by his distaste ...' the expressions of anti-Catholicism than his concern for the risk of fire. For ...:se Lewes clerics the immorality and irreligiosity that they associated with the ...lebrations stimulated their opposition.

...The four bonfire societies were represented at the subcommittee hearings by ...ding members including A. W. Hillman of Southover, J. W. Briggs of Cliffe, ...T. Gearing of Borough and P. W. King and S. J. Stevenson of Commercial Square.

They attempted to counter criticism by asserting that the celebrations were a goo advertisement for Lewes and promoted trade, a large amount of money bein brought into the town by visitors who had come to witness the celebrations. Hug Vinall, a local solicitor, also speaking on behalf of the societies at the hearin commended the celebrations as 'loyal, Protestant, orderly, and religious an conducted with marked sobriety'. His membership of the Loyal Orange Lodge ma however explain his support for the Bonfire Boys.

Leading Lewesians also rallied to the support of the societies. William Baxte through his editorial in the Express, commented favourably on the character o the Bonfire Boys while Alderman George Holman expressed his support at th unlikely venue of the Annual Football Club Dinner. In his Presidential addres he observed how many of the old English sports have fallen into abeyance owin principally in his opinion to the platitudes and sophistry of 'goody-goody peopl Holman was the antithesis of Kemp. He too, as a director of Baxters, was businessman, a past Mayor and a County Councillor, but he was a staunc Conservative and patron of many local sporting and social associations. His suppo for the Bonfire Boys led to the indignity of having his house searched by Hon Office inspectors looking for explosives used in the manufacture of firework

On 17th April, 1906 the Joint Standing Committee received the sub-committee report and took the decision to prohibit the throwing of fireworks and the makin of street fires, which although illegal had previously been tolerated. Notice publicising this decision were to be posted and the bonfire societies informe The Express lamented this decision claiming that the celebrations as Lewesia knew them would be no more. The Bonfire Boys were uncertain whether to contin the celebrations at all, some regarding the 'Fifth' without fires, tar barrels, ar Lewes Rousers to be a very tame affair, while others thought some effort shou be made to provide an evening's amusement. The societies finally agreed to ho processions in their own areas of the town before joining in a combined processic to a site on the outskirts of the town where a large bonfire and firework displa would be held.

These initial plans however were not carried out, in the event the societies acti independently of each other. Southover and Borough experienced considerab difficulties. Southover, unable to find an alternative firesite, suspended operatio Borough, in addition to losing financial support causing the Society to run in debt, were unable to find a firesite. Rather than disband they entered into a form amalgamation with Commercial Square, to form the 'Commercial Square a Borough Bonfire Society'. In return for Commercial Square honouring their det the Borough agreed not to reorganise as a separate Society for a period of thr years. The Commercial Square had already been promised the use of a field alo the Brighton Road by Richard Brown, a local farmer, and Francis Verral J.P. T Cliffe was least affected, moving its firesite onto Malling Fields, not far from Clii High Street.

The police mustered 130 men in Lewes for the 'Fifth' in 1906 to ensure t

County Council's instructions were upheld. Seventeen men were arrested including four leading members of Commercial Square, William Gearing, his son Thomas, Eli Dawe and Harold Weston. They were charged with participating in an unlawful assembly in Commercial Square during which an attempt was made to build a fire. Divergent evidence given by the police and numerous defence witnesses led to the accused being discharged, a result made the sweeter by the fact that the magistrate compelled to acquit them was their arch opponent Caleb Rickman Kemp. On leaving the court, the four were carried shoulder high down the street amidst a cheering crowd.

In the following years the Police remained vigilant, again responding firmly in 1911 when the Bonfire Boys tested their resolve by dragging blazing tar barrels on a trolley cart through the streets, the police responding by arresting six Commercial Square members. On this occasion the authorities acted leniently, the summonses being withdrawn on condition the Bonfire Boys acknowledged the illegality of their actions. Apart from these brushes with the law the Bonfire Boys continued their activities within the parameters set by the Committee's decision until the outbreak fo the First World War when the celebrations were suspended for the duration of the war.

EAST SUSSEX CONSTABULARY
5th NOVEMBER CELEBRATIONS.
UNLAWFUL ASSEMBLIES.

WHEREAS it is unlawful for any persons to assemble with the object of carrying out any common purpose, lawful or unlawful, in such a manner as to give other persons reason to fear a disturbance of the peace.

NOTICE IS HEREBY GIVEN that any persons who assemble for the purpose of lighting or attempting to light Bonfires in the streets, or setting fire or attempting to set fire to Fireworks or Tar Barrels in the streets, or throwing lighted Torches in or about the streets, or doing any other act which may be reasonably expected to create or tend to the creation of a disturbance of the Peace will be arrested by virtue of the powers vested in the Police for arresting persons taking part in an unlawful assembly.

Dated this 1st day of November, 1907.

HUGH G. LANG, Bt. Major,
Chief Constable.

A 1907 Police notice clearly stating the parameters in which the Bonfire Boys could conduct their celebrations following the County Council Joint Standing Committee's decision to prohibit fires, fireworks and tar barrels in the street.

43

7. THE BONFIRE BOYS AND THEIR SUPPORTERS

Before describing events following the war certain characteristics of the nineteenth century bonfire societies and their membership may be touched upon to illustrate the underlying dynamics present among them and how these have changed in the present century.

As their names suggest the bonfire societies were based in areas of the town from which they took their names. This neighbourhood orientation was manifest from the time of their formation, the 'Town' west of the river in Lewes itself, the 'Cliffe' to the east in the suburb of Cliffe. Prior to the First World War the Commercial Square, Waterloo and South Street Juvenile Bonfire Societies each took their names from streets while Southover and St Anne's from parishes of the same name. A number of other minor short-lived associations of Bonfire Boys originating from the activities of juveniles also manifest the same neighbourhood orientation. These included in 1859 the 'Rising Generation' of Chapel-hill Bonfire Boys, in 1870 the South-street Bonfire Society, in 1872 the St Michael's Society and in 1892 the Sun Street Juveniles and Toronto Terrace Boys. A 'St Johns Star Society' also existed in St John's Street immediately prior to the First World War.

The societies acknowledged the territorial basis of their activities confining their procession routes, firesite, headquarters, street collections and recruitment to their own neighbourhood. The Express captured the spirit in which the notion of territory was held by the Bonfire Boys when it observed that the 'Bonfire Boys are quite as jealous of their territory as masters of hounds, and the Cliffe Society would no more think of marching in procession on the West side of Lewes Bridge, than the worthy master of the Southdown Hounds would contemplate drawing a covert belonging to a neighbouring hunt'. One particular incident graphically illustrates this. The Borough had traditionally processed through Southover High Street and did not cease to do so until 1896, ten years after the formation of Southover Bonfire Society. Following the disbandment of Southover in 1906 Cliffe processed the full extent of the now unoccupied territory of Southover High Street. However at Borough's re-formation meeting in 1909 the secretary, F. H. Gearing, reported having approached Cliffe requesting the restoration of Southover territory to Borough. The Cliffe did not respond immediately, but in 1910 the Society ceased to march through Southover High Street leaving Borough to 're-occupy' their former territory.

Such was the community spirit among Bonfire Boys that it was not unusual for them to come to the aid of fellow Bonfire Boys or their families in times of need, financial aid frequently being organised to assist individual members meet the expense of hiring defence lawyers in court cases. This had occurred at the time of the riots and was again repeated in 1906 and 1911 when Bonfire Boys were arrested following police crackdowns on aspects of their activities. Similarly in times of individual hardship Bonfire Boys rallied round as in 1909 when Tom Gearing, a Commercial Square torchman, died as a result of being badly burnt

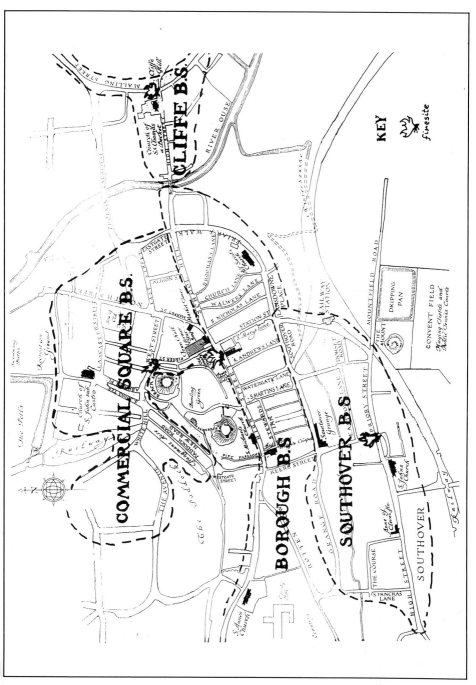

The town of Lewes indicating the firesites and territories of the four societies existing before the outbreak of World War One. The territories are based upon the societies' processional routes and recruitment areas.

while 'running' torches. A subscription list set up to help his family raised £183.3s.10d. In 1913 the Cliffe held a 'smoker' to raise money for a member who was unable to work due to having broken his leg.

Since the Second World War two new societies have been formed, Landport in 1948 and Nevill Juvenile in 1968. The Waterloo Bonfire Society, previously existing briefly during the latter half of the nineteenth century was resurrected in 1964. While Landport and Nevill followed the traditional pattern of activity and recruitment by processing through the streets and recruiting from the two housing estates from which they took their names the Waterloo had less of an affinity with territory drawing members from the entire town and from the other societies. However it is Waterloo that typifies contemporary bonfire societies, the old established societies no longer processing exclusively within their original territories nor relying on neighbourhood recruitment for their membership. Today's members are drawn largely from among friends and family, recruitment now being dependent on social contact rather than territorial considerations.

One reason for this change is undoubtedly the growing strength of today's societies, the larger ones having two to three hundred 'paid up' members. The

Southover Bonfire Society, 1905. Among the costumed members are Colonial and Japanese soldiers. The Colonials were the Society's pioneers while the Japanese contingent complemented the tableau, 'A Russian Incident', which referred to the Russo-Japanese War. J. Tyrell Glandfield, the 'Lord High Chancellor of Southover', is seated in the centre in ermine trimmed robes. The banner bears the Society's motto, 'Advance Southover', which was adopted some fourteen years earlier.

Commercial Square Bonfire Society, 1908. On the extreme left and right, dressed in the traditional Guernseys are the Society's torchmakers, while the 'Archbishop', Harry G. Cruse is seated in the front row. The banner on the left bears the Society's badge comprising of two crossed torches.

Lewes Borough Bonfire Society during the 1890s. The Society's leading figure, W. T. Gearing, attired in clerical regalia is seated among the costumed members. The key held aloft at the back is the 'Ancient Key of the Borough of Lewes'. It symbolises the Bonfire Boys belief that they enjoyed the 'freedom of the town' on Bonfire Night.

membership of the nineteenth century societies was small by comparison, probably numbering a little over one hundred. According to press reports processions range from '70 marching four deep' in the Cliffe in 1862 to 160 in the Commercial Square's 1893 Grand Procession. Commercial Square announced membership numbers at their Annual Dinner, in 1896, the secretary reporting 140 members, 59 committee and 81 general. This number remained fairly constant, in 1906 the Society's strength standing at 45 committee and 93 general, a total of 138 members.

The general membership of the societies was drawn largely from the town's young male working class population, the term 'Bonfire Boys' reflecting their age and perhaps their behaviour. First coined by the Advertiser when describing those involved in the 1827 celebrations the term, joined more recently by 'Bonfire Girls', has become synonymous with all those Lewesians involved in the celebrations. However the membership was not drawn exclusively from this group. The societies received considerable support from owners of small manufacturing or retailing businesses. Among those holding leading positions in the societies immediately before the First World War were William Alfred Hillman, a master grocer trading

Cliffe Bonfire Society circa 1908. Indian princes had been the Society's pioneers since 1904, but reference to the banner 'Success to the Bonfire Society' was first made in 1908. The indistinct banner on the left depicts the 'Discovery of Guy Fawkes'. Both banners were carried throughout the inter-war years but were subsequently lost.

South Street Juvenile Bonfire Society, 1913. A group of children in fancy dress pose in front of Willes Cottages in South Street. On the extreme left is Tom Wheeler, the Society's founding member.

in Southover High Street, James Urry, a furniture dealer and coal merchant also of Southover, George Trayton Baker, a baker and confectioner of St Anne's, Percy Wood King, a general dealer of North Street, and Stanley John Stevenson, one of three brothers in the family North Street business of corn and seed merchants who were all active in Commercial Square.

One man in particular stands out as the 'respectable' image of Bonfire at the turn of the century. William Thomas Gearing, Borough's 'Bishop' for over forty years was a substantial individual. He moved from London with his parents during the 1840s and spent his working life with the printing firm of Baxters, first as a compositor, then later as the firm's collector. Politically a Conservative and a member of the Loyal Orange Lodge, he was associated with a number of local voluntary associations including the Ancient Order of Buffalos, Foresters and Oddfellows, Lewes Football Club, Rowing Club and Operatic Society. He belonged to some for a considerable time, being a chorister at All Saints for forty years and Colour Sergeant in the Rifle Volunteers, from which he retired in 1898 after 33 years service. His obituary and funeral arrangements in July 1913 reflected the esteem in which he was held. Members of 'D' Company 5th Royal Sussex Regiment headed the funeral cortege and he was laid to rest with full military honours, including a graveside firing party.

The societies also attracted more eccentric local characters to their ranks. One

William Thomas Gearing in top hat and clerical robes posed as if haranguing the crowds. He wears the sash of the Loyal Orange Institution of which he was a member. This photograph appeared in the December 1905 edition of 'The Protestant Times'.

(Photo: B. Reeves)

such was John Newton who, like Gearing, had been a Borough 'Bishop'. Born in Lewes in 1821 Newton was a successful High Street tobacconist during his early life, but later his fortunes declined, ending his working days making paper bags and hawking oranges and nuts at the railway station. Newton died in the workhouse infirmary at the age of 62 having been in bad health, physically and mentally for some time. His obituary in 1883 describes him as a 'local celebrity' of unsettled character, arranging "dramatic" entertainment in cellars of houses and appearing attired in an extraordinary manner that attracted public notice. He had been the Borough's 'Bishop' during its formative years, but according to the Express he 'got into bad odour with the members, and was afterwards looked upon as a traitor to the cause'.

The Bonfire Boys' cause was undoubtedly strengthened by the 'respectable' element active in the societies. From having been labelled the 'mob', the formation of the bonfire societies, the organisation of the celebrations into a more acceptable form, and the open recruitment of many leading men of the town enabled the Bonfire Boys to take on an air of respectability. Their annual dinners bear witness to this new found social image, with guest speakers, including the Mayor or town councillors, proposing a whole series of loyal and patriotic toasts. This support continued after the war, each societies' programmes containing long lists of vice presidents and subscribers which included many from the local business community. Leading Lewesians have also been Presidents of the societies. For many years a local G.P. and one time Mayor, Dr Pat Nicholl, was President of the Borough while Reg Yarrow, Borough Mayor and first Chairman of the newly formed Lewes District Council was Cliffe's President during the 1970s and 80s.

Similarly their involvement in the town's organising committees for royal and civic occasions continues to enhance their acceptability and promote good relations between themselves and the town. In 1953 the societies organised the torchlit procession, a 30ft high tableau of the Barbican Gateway and a beacon fire on Cliffe Hill to celebrate the Coronation of Queen Elizabeth II. Twenty four years on the Bonfire Boys led the townspeople in procession through the town from their street parties to the Grand Firework Display on Malling Brooks to mark the occasion of the Queen's Silver Jubilee. Members of the Borough along with other Sussex Carnival Societies travelled to Windsor Great Park to mark the occasion in the presence of the Queen.

The societies also became fully involved in the town's festivities to mark the 700th Anniversary of the Battle of Lewes in 1964, the torchlit procession and firework display again being organised by the societies. In more recent years the bonfire societies have become involved in twinning activities between Lewes and its two twin towns in Europe. They travelled to France in 1973 where they provided the now customary torchlit procession through the town of Blois, in the Loire Valley, as part of the festivities to commemorate the 10th Anniversary of twinning between Lewes and Blois. In 1988 the societies again travelled to Europe, this time to Waldshut-Tiengen, Lewes's German twin town, where they participated in a traditional German carnival.

8. THE INTER-WAR YEARS, 1919-1938

Following the cessation of hositilities in November 1918 the Bonfire Boys became fully involved in the preparations for the town's Armistice Procession. Under the chairmanship of Councillor Frank Taylor, a Commercial Square member, a committee including representatives of all the town's bonfire societies was hurriedly set up to make the necessary arrangements for a torchlit procession. Led by the Band of the Royal Sussex Regiment the procession left the Swan, Southover, at seven o'clock on 20th November 1918 to parade through the streets of Lewes. Among the processionists were costumed Bonfire Boys carrying a large banner inscribed with the motto 'To the Memory of Our Bonfire Boys who have fallen in the War'.

The societies were however slower to rekindle their zest to celebrate the Discovery of the Gunpowder Plot. Only Cliffe mustered sufficient support to revive the Bonfire Night celebrations in 1919. The Society had kept in touch with members throughout the war years, sending Christmas cards to men on active service. Having established their headquarters at the Dorset Arms the Cliffe acquired a firesite on Malling Hill where, on the 'Fifth' they showed their disdain for their German enemies by exploding a Grand Tableau entitled 'Kaiser Bill's Ride To London'. The following year saw the first street collections being made for charitable purposes, the recipient being St Dunstan's Hostel for Blind Soldiers. This remained the Society's chosen

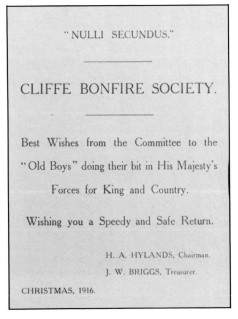

The front and inside of the 1916 Christmas cards sent from the Cliffe Society to its members serving in the forces during the First World War. Similar cards exist for 1915 and 1917.

charity until 1930 when the money raised was donated to Lewes Victoria Hospital. Following their reformation the other societies followed Cliffe's lead and over the years large sums have been raised annually for local charities.

It was not until 1921 that other societies began to revive the spirit of 'Bonfire' in their areas of the town. In that year Borough set up their firesite in the Ham, off Southover High Street and were led by the Brighton Tramways Band for their first processions since the war. South Street Juveniles also commenced operations with a fire at the end of South Street. The following year Commercial Square reformed, holding their fire in a stubble field at Landport. By 1923 Southover had recommenced activities followed by St Anne's in 1926.

Although there had been a break in proceedings due to the war the celebrations themselves remained largely unaltered, the only significant change being the introduction of the Bonfire Boys' Remembrance Service at the War Memorial. Initially this ceremony was kept separate from the celebrations. Following the erection of the town's War Memorial in 1922 the Cliffe mustered at Headquarters on the Sunday afternoon prior to the 'Fifth' before proceeding to the Memorial to lay a wreath and sound the 'Last Post' in memory of those who had died during the war. They were joined by Commercial Square in the following year with Southover and Borough holding a similar service the following day. This act of 'Remembrance' soon became an integral part of each society's programme on the 'Fifth'. In 1926 the Borough marched to the War Memorial with the band playing the Death March before laying their wreath and observing a minute's silence. By 1927 Southover was holding a similar ceremony at the War Memorial outside of Southover Church.

Other changes during this period were more gradual and less perceptible. Bonfire Night appears to have been a male preserve prior to the war. Although women were participating as early as 1867 when 'some young women, not to be outdone by their sweethearts' were observed 'donned in fanciful attire' in Borough's procession. More regular involvement appears not to have occurred until much later in the century. In the 1890s women were leading the processions, marching among the lancers of the Borough's and Cliffe's pioneers. In the years immediately prior to the war women frequently entered the fancy dress competitions held by the Commercial Square at the Elephant and Castle and by 1911 a ladies class had been introduced. But while a number of female clerics were attending the "Lord Bishop of the Cliffe" at the firesite in 1905 women appear not to have held any positions of importance in the societies' hierarchies.

However this situation started to change following the war when female participation increased with many more women appearing in photographs of costumed groups of society members. It was during this period that women became accepted onto the societies' committees. In a letter to the secretary of Cliffe in 1935, A. E. Faithful, an 'old Bonfire Boy and one time Chairman' of the Society who had emigrated to Kenya commented that he thought 'the introduction of the ladies of the Society into the General Meetings and on the Committee is a step

The wreath laying ceremony at the town's War Memorial in 1978. Two trumpeters of the Band of the Staffordshire Regiment sound the Last Post while the President of the Cliffe prepares to lay the wreath.
(Photo: Sussex Express)

St Anne's Bonfire Society sometime between 1926 and 1938. The members are dressed in the Valencian costume of the Society's pioneers. The large number of women in this group indicates their increasing involvement in the celebrations following the First World War.

in the right direction and should enhance the social side of the meetings'. Perhaps a little patronizing for the modern feminist his words none-the-less bear witness to the increasing role of women in the organisation of the societies and the celebrations. This trend has continued, many of the principle committee officers of today's societies being women.

A second gradual but far more observable change occurring during the inter-war years was the relationship of co-operation that existed among the bonfire societies. A competitive spirit between the societies had always been present, but so too had the desire to co-operate with each other especially when there was a threat to their celebrations, as in 1905. This was the attitude between them in 1930 when the first Combined Procession organised by the District Council of Lewes Bonfire Societies created the spectacle that many Lewesians had been calling for. The idea for such a procession had first been mooted at a meeting of representatives from Borough, Southover, Commercial Square and South Street in 1923, but no agreement could be reached at that time. However, following a plea by Captain Hawkes Reed, President of the Commercial Square at the Society's annual dinner in 1929 the procession took place. Led through the High Street by Cliffe it was supported by all six Lewes societies. In a similar spirit of co-operation three years earlier Cliffe and Borough had met at the bottom of School Hill at eleven o'clock to sing 'Auld Lang Syne', so reviving a custom that had lapsed since 1905.

Commercial Square's tableau in 1924 was entitled 'Wanted. A Closed Gate'. Designed and constructed by C. W. and G. F. Geering it represents a German commercial traveller standing before the closed gate of Britain with a bag of samples in his hand and a stock of goods behind him. G. F. Geering is the slightly lower central figure.

But this harmony was short lived. In 1931 Cliffe resigned from the Council and took no further part in the combined procession. This break marked the beginning of a long running feud between Cliffe and the other societies. Following the war Cliffe had revived the practice of burning the effigy of Pope Paul V signifying their intention to retain the strong anti-Catholic tradition that had typified the nineteenth century celebrations. But attitudes towards Roman Catholics were changing. Catholics and Protestants had fought as comrades throughout the war and for many the distrust of Roman Catholics that had prevailed during the past was now considered irrelevant. Reflecting this change in mood Borough replaced their papal effigy by one of Catesby in 1923, Commercial Square burnt only Guy Fawkes and in 1926 Southover announced that they were discontinuing the final verse of the 'Bonfire Prayers'.

Responding to this change in mood and as a result of having received letters criticising the Cliffe's continuing practice of burning the papal effigy the then Mayor, J. C. Kenward, in November 1933 wrote to the Society's Chairman, H. Woolley, requesting that Cliffe should discontinue what was considered by many to be offensive. The Cliffe declined and in the following year its clergy accused the other societies of coming perilously near to degrading the celebrations to the level of mere carnival, a point emphasised by their tableau of that year which depicted

Pope Paul V in bed with Guy Fawkes. The other societies appear to have responded to this taunt, Commercial Square burning a papal effigy in 1935, Borough doing likewise the following year, the first time since the war. But while the societies were at loggerheads the clouds of war were looming. In 1938 the tableaux had a prophetic theme, each in their own way foreseeing what was to come. Borough's tableau was entitled 'Make Britain Strong, Its Yours, Be Prepared to Guard it Well'; Southover, 'Somewhere in England' portraying a village being bombed; Commercial Square, 'Should We Have Told Them To Go?', comprising of large effigies representing Hitler, Mussolini and the Devil; and Cliffe, 'The Eruption of Europe' symbolically depicted in the form of a huge volcano.

The Borough tableau of 1925, a model of Cliffe Bridge and entitled 'This Year, Next Year, Sometime — Never', drew attention to the dilatoriness of the town and county authorities to agree on how best to enlarge the bridge. Designed by Sydney 'Bert' Munt (third from right) the tableau is unusual in that it comments on a local issue.

"Still With Us", the 1928 Cliffe tableau, was constructed by A. Briggs (Indian Prince) and W. Fielder (Clown) and represented the desired fate of D.O.R.A. The Bonfire Boys always championed liberal licensing laws so were opposed to the continued restriction on the hours of drinking imposed by the Defence of the Realm Act.

The Borough procession passing County Hall in 1938 accompanied by the Buxted Silver Band which was ostentatiously described in the programme as 'The Society's Celebrated Military Prize Band'. The procession is led by cavaliers, the Society's pioneers in the years prior to the outbreak of World War Two.

9. POST-WAR TRENDS

Following the Second World War the societies were quick to recommence the celebrations, Cliffe, Borough, Commercial Square and South Street all organising celebrations in 1945. These societies have since flourished, each holding their individual annual celebrations since their reformation except in 1960 when severe flooding in Lewes caused the only peace time cancellation. Southover reformed in 1950, but the Society's revival was short lived, disbanding eight years later through lack of support. A new society, Landport, met a similar fate, forming in 1948 but surviving only six years. Two other new societies have fared better. Waterloo, resurrected in 1964, joined the established societies and quickly became one of the town's leading societies. In 1968 Nevill Juvenile Bonfire Society was also formed, its expressed purpose to provide the youngsters living on Nevill Estate the opportunity of becoming involved in 'Bonfire'. Unlike the other societies Nevill hold their celebrations on a Saturday prior to the 'Fifth' joining with one of the other societies on Bonfire Night.

Probably the most significant feature of the celebrations following the Second World War is their unchanging form which remains basically that which was adopted after the banning of street fires in 1906 with the addition of the 'Remembrance' at the War Memorial. To the casual observer the only changes now occurring are the subjects of the societies' tableaux, the occasional new pioneer front of one or two of the societies and minor modifications to processional routes due to changes of firesites.

The Southover Bonfire Society processing down Southover High Street during the early 1950s. The members dressed as Indian princes, the Society's pioneer costume, precede the large banner 'Advance Southover' which depicts the Landing of William of Orange. (Photo: Sussex Express)

The unchanging character of the celebrations is typified by the pioneers of the Commercial Square Bonfire Society. Red Indians were first mentioned specifically as the Society's pioneers in 1909 and they have remained so through to the present day. Here Indian chieftains lead the Society during the early 1960s.
(Photo: E. A. Meyer)

But there have been changes. Cliffe stubbornly maintain the 'No Popery' tradition of the celebrations, continuing to burn the effigy of Paul V. But while they claim to be burning the effigy of the Pope at the time of the Gunpowder Plot and therefore a traditional effigy that has no contemporary relevance the Society still provokes frequent criticism both nationally and locally. Writing in the Daily Sketch in 1959 John Knight referred to the 'hatred underlying the laughs' and the presence of 'an ugly undercurrent of religious fanaticism' that he had observed at the Lewes celebrations. In 1970 the Sunday People headline 'Bigots around the Bonfire' succinctly summarised its report. During the 1970s the local Catholic priest was often critical, his comments provoking a sizeable correspondence in the local press. Cliffe's rebuttal of the more extreme of these criticisms however signifies a shift in sentiment underlying the burning of the papal effigy. No longer a contemporary comment as it had been in the nineteenth century the offending effigy has now become an intrinsic element, along with many others, of what many Bonfire Boys perceive as the true traditions of 'Bonfire'.

This issue has until very recently continued to divide the societies. Immediately after the Second World War Cliffe sent delegates to the Combined Bonfire Society meetings but by 1948 had withdrawn due to the 'No Popery' issue. In 1954 they refused an invitation from the Bonfire Council to join the other Lewes societies in the Combined Procession. The Cliffe's refusal was caused by the Council's offer being conditional on the 'No Popery' banner not being carried in the procession. The Council made a second unconditional invitation to join the 'Combined' in 1961, but again Cliffe refused. The Lewes Bonfire Council had been established in 1948 by Borough, Commercial Square, Landport and South Street Juveniles to co-ordinate their activities. The Cliffe did rejoin the Council in 1972, but while the Society plays a full part in its activities, the present Council secretary and a predecessor both being Cliffe members, Cliffe has retained its independent spirit by continuing to march alone on the 'Fifth'.

It is the traditions of the 'Fifth', so closely observed by the Bonfire Boys, that set 'Bonfire' apart from mere 'Carnival'. To an outsider the distinction may appear insignificant, but among the Bonfire Boys the difference is of considerable importance. For them 'Bonfire' defines all that is traditional about their activities, the commemoration of historical events, the recalling of past religious antagonism and the intrinsic rituals, developed since the formation of the societies, that are now firmly established as part of their celebrations. This sense of tradition is strongly

Zulus have long been associated with the Borough Society, the costume being adopted as the Society's pioneer group soon after the Second World War. The central figure with the tall head dress is Ted Over, a leading member of the Borough during the 1960s and 70s. (Photo: Sussex Express)

The Ghengis Khan warriors of the Waterloo Bonfire Society have been the Society's pioneer costume since 1969. The banner depicts the 'Bonfire Boys' Arms' copied from a small wooden plaque dating from the nineteenth century.

(Photo: Sussex Express)

The Viking costume of the Cliffe Society, first introduced in 1951, does not have the extended pedigree of the Red Indian or Zulu. Scots and later Cavaliers have for short periods replaced the Vikings as the leading processionist but in recent years the costume has established itself as the favoured choice of the members. (Photo: Leigh Simpson)

South Street Juvenile Bonfire Society starts them young. Wearing the costume of the Siamese dancers, for a long time the Society's pioneers, these four children are accompanied by their mother in the procession.

(Photo: Sussex Express)

held by the contemporary Bonfire Boys, any innovation not considered to be in keeping with tradition being roundly criticised. In this spirit the use of loud speaker vans or the participation of Morris dancers in processions has met with disapproval while the introduction of 'barrel carts', ninety-gallon drums cut in half, mounted on wheels, filled with burning torches and pulled through the streets in imitation of the nineteenth century barrels, is perfectly acceptable.

But while the bonfire societies strive to maintain the traditional form of the 'Fifth' in Lewes changes are being imposed on them that are altering the character and spirit of their celebrations. In the past local incidents have provided the catalyst for change, as in 1847 and 1906. More recently pressure for change has been the consequence of traffic, changing social attitudes and national events. Some have been to the advantage of the celebrations, but others appear to pose a threat and are being resisted by the societies.

Before the First World War very few motor cars were seen in Lewes and probably none on the 'Fifth', but traffic became an increasing problem between the wars. As early as 1927 the police were making strenuous efforts to regulate the flow of traffic to allow processions to pass unimpeded. Parked cars posed their own particular difficulties, being used as grandstands in the High Street in 1935. This problem increased after the Second World War as the volume of through traffic was swelled by increasing numbers of spectators arriving by car. Parking restrictions eased the situation on processional routes but the problem was not resolved until the opening of the Lewes Bypass enabled the High Street and other main processional routes to be closed to traffic throughout the evening.

Drinking and an element of drunkenness had always been present during the celebrations and by the mid 1960s the behaviour of some among the large numbers of young people attending the celebrations as spectators was causing concern. On the advice of the police the town's public houses begun to close their doors, and by the 1970s all town centre pubs were tightly shut on the 'Fifth'. The removal of the more lively from among the crowds had a significant consequence that was not initially acknowledged. As the rowdiness associated with Lewes Bonfire Night declined so the numbers of families among the spectators increased. From their point of view Bonfire Night has become a much tamer affair.

This 'taming' of the celebrations has also gradually removed the street fireworks so long associated with the 'Fifth'. The original 'Lewes Rouser', a large homemade squib that sent the crowds scurrying for cover as it shot across the ground was replaced following the First World War by manufactured squibs and 'bangers' which were thrown with abandon in the crowded streets. Confiscation of the offending rockets or arrest by the police occurred annually and their persistence, backed by harsher penalties and legislation restricting the sale of fireworks has resulted in this practice being almost totally eliminated. Similar restrictions have been imposed on the societies. Small firework displays, referred to as 'setpieces', are ignited in the processions at certain times during the evening's ceremonies, many at the War Memorial Remembrance. In recent years the size and type of fireworks used in the setpieces have been strictly regulated.

Many of these changes have been motivated by concern for public safety and while very few serious injuries have occurred since the fatality in 1909 the authorities have remained vigilant. The Hillsborough disaster has prompted the most recent re-appraisal of public safety and policing of large public gatherings. This has had a direct consequence for the celebrations with the authorities attempting to impose stringent regulations on the bonfire societies in 1992. Those relating to crowd safety at the firework displays may be viewed as constructive, but the societies are resisting the implementation of other regulations that will affect the conduct of their processions, considering them unnecessary and impractical impositions.

'Enemies of Bonfire', 1992   (Photo: Phil Everitt)

10. A SURVIVING TRADITION

Having arrived back at the present day the questions posed at the beginning of this account of the Lewes Bonfire Night celebrations may now be considered. First the rather simplistic and erroneous explanations so frequently given for the survival of the celebrations must be dispensed with. The celebration's survival is frequently attributed to the fact that during the nineteenth century Lewes had been a centre of religious nonconformity. This is certainly true, numerous nonconformist sects with large congregations flourishing in the town. But the assumption that the survival of the celebrations was a result of support given to the Bonfire Boys by the nonconformists because of the celebrations anti-Catholic manifestations is based on a misunderstanding. As has been shown it was from among the ranks of these sects that the most fervent opponents of the celebrations were drawn, the issues of morality and sobriety over-riding consideration of doctrinal differences between themselves and Roman Catholics. In today's more secular society it is doubtful if any religious grouping is having an influence on the celebrations, and certainly not sufficient to account for their survival.

Lewes being the scene of martyrdom during the Marian persecutions is often linked with the previous explanation. But while the burning of the seventeen protestant martyrs had occurred in the middle of the sixteenth century it was not until the erection of the Martyrs' Memorial on Cliffe Hill in 1901 that the martyrdom was regularly acknowledged by the Bonfire Boys. As has been described, the nineteenth century Bonfire Boys were more concerned with contemporary religious issues rather than past ones. Today, even though the Lewes Martyrs are remembered on the 'Fifth', this is only one of many traditional features of the celebrations and again certainly contributes little to their survival.

For more tenable explananations it is necessary to seek the answers from the celebrations and the activities of the Bonfire Boys themselves. Attention has been drawn to the fact that while the 'Fifth' was legally a day of rejoicing it also enjoyed considerable financial and moral support from the Conservative gentry and businessmen of the town, support that enabled the Bonfire Boys to resist attempts to suppress their celebrations. The continued support from this section of the community, although no longer politically motivated has undoubtedly helped to sustain the celebrations. Successful suppression during the nineteenth century or more recent decline has been experienced in many towns where such support has not been forthcoming.

One explanation for the continued support enjoyed by the Lewes Bonfire Boys during the nineteenth century was the lack of rapid urban development of the town. Unlike many towns in the south east Lewes remained a small market town serving its rural hinterland throughout the nineteenth and into the twentieth century. In expanding places like Brighton, Guildford, Horsham and Tunbridge Wells the celebrations were quickly suppressed once they posed a threat to the economic and social development of the town. While such concerns were expressed by opponents to the celebrations in Lewes their arguments had little influence and as time passed such fears proved to be unfounded. As a result the social climate became increasingly more tolerant towards the celebrations.

During the nineteenth century support from within each of the neighbourhoods for their bonfire society must also have sustained the celebrations. Residents who became involved identified with their society and the sense of community generated by its adherence to a defined territory. The 'Fifth' provided the Bonfire Boys with an opportunity to express their loyalty both to the Society and their community. As membership of societies was sustained through their continued existence so a tradition of family membership evolved which further ensured the survival of the society. Today there are many who can show family membership with a society spreading both through and across generations. Nor should the pleasure derived from this social interaction between members be overlooked as a contributing factor to the survival of the celebrations. Bonfire Night was and is a night of fun, when the inhabitants can enjoy a release from their everyday humdrum lives. It provides an opportunity for family get-togethers and for members to renew old acquaintances. For the active member the Society can also provide a full social life, with regular committee meetings, fund-raising and social events.

The competitive spirit existing between the societies also generates an inter-society dynamic that fosters their survival. Members wish their society to be the best, to have the biggest membership, the longest processions, the best costumes and the most spectacular firework display. They will strive to achieve this and in so doing strengthen the celebrations by way of promoting their own society. Today the Bonfire Council organises an annual Fancy Dress Competition just prior to Bonfire Night, the various classes being keenly contested between the societies. In a different way the dispute over the 'No Popery' issue generates a similar competitive edge between the societies.

The celebrations have always had a purpose, and while this purpose has changed over the years it has helped to give a reason for maintaining the celebrations. During the nineteenth century the celebrations were used as a vehicle to promote religious and political views, providing many who were not enfranchised an opportunity to publicly express themselves on these issues. While this aspect of the celebrations has declined their longevity has allowed traditions to evolve which in themselves provide reason for continuing the celebrations. Just as the early Bonfire Boys wished to retain their customal rights today's Bonfire Boys are aware that they are perpetuating a celebration that has existed in Lewes for well over two centuries. They are conscious that if they are to survive then the traditions of the 'Fifth' must be maintained and passed on to the next generation of Bonfire Boys.

The future survival of the celebrations is in part dependent on the continuing recruitment of the next generation. A family group dressed as cavaliers here stand below a banner portraying the Gunpowder Plot conspirators. (Photo: Sussex Express)

APPENDIX

Society Chairpersons/Secretaries (at the time of publication)

If you require further information about the activities of today's Lewes bonfire societies or wish to become a member of one of them they may be contacted through either the societies' chairpersons or secretaries.

Cliffe Bonfire Society
Bryan Parrott, Waterloo House, Waterloo Place, Lewes BN7 2PP

Commercial Square Bonfire Society
John Richards, 33 Hereward Way, Lewes

Lewes Borough Bonfire Society
David Winter, 25 Mountharry Road, Lewes BN7 1NU

Nevill Juvenile Bonfire Society
Anne Stephenson, 33 Priory Street, Lewes

South Street Juvenile Bonfire Society
Barbara Nichols, 23 Buckhurst Close, Lewes BN7 2ES

Waterloo Bonfire Society
Christine Jackman, 4 The Meadows, Lewes

Lewes Bonfire Council
Keith Austin, 25b Priory Street, Lewes BN7 1HH

ACKNOWLEDGEMENTS

Sincere thanks are due to the following for permission to use photographs or documents in their possession: Cliffe Bonfire Society, Commercial Square Bonfire Society, South Street Juvenile Bonfire Society, Waterloo Bonfire Society, Sussex Archaeological Society, Lewes Public Library and Brian Beckingham. Especial thanks are due to the Sussex Express, Phil Burcham, Phil Everitt, E. A. Meyer, Edward Reeves, Leigh Simpson and Pete Varnham for permission to use photographs from their collections.

My gratitude for help is also due to the staff of East Sussex Record Office and Sussex Archaeological Society, and to individual Bonfire Boys, Pete Martin, Dave Quinn, Bruce Wadey and David Winter who assisted in locating some of the illustrations.

Finally a special thankyou is due to Sue Etherington for reading through the final draft to correct the inevitable careless errors.

THE AUTHOR

Jim Etherington was born in Lewes in 1947. He graduated with a B.Ed. in Education and Sociology from the University of Sussex, later becoming a part-time graduate student with the Open University, gaining his Ph.D. in 1988.

As a child he observed the Lewes Bonfire Night celebrations with his parents as a spectator before joining the Cliffe Bonfire Society in his early teens. He served on the Society's committee for over twenty years latterly as Treasurer and Secretary. For a number of years he was also Treasurer, then Secretary of the Lewes Bonfire Council.

Jim Etherington is a teacher currently working in Haywards Heath. He is married with two teenage children.

AUTHOR'S NOTE

In recent years each bonfire society has come to realise the importance of maintaining a record of their own history by compiling an archive of photographs, press cuttings, programmes and other miscellany pertaining to their society. If a reader has any such material that they would like to donate or lend for copying please contact the relevant society secretary listed at the end of this book.

Zulus of Lewes Borough Bonfire Society